THE DONVIER® ICE CREAM DESSERT BOOK

D1023741

THE DONVIER® ICE CREAM DESSERT BOOK

By Anna Creery

THE
DONNING COMPANY
PUBLISHERS
NORFOLK/VIRGINIA BEACH

Copyright © 1988 by Nikkal Industries, Ltd.

All rights reserved, including the right to reproduce this work in any form whatsoever without permission in writing from the publisher, except for brief passages in connection with a review. For information, write:

The Donning Company/Publishers
5659 Virginia Beach Boulevard
Norfolk, Virginia 23502

Library of Congress Cataloging-in-Publication Data

Creery, Anna A.
The Donvier ice cream dessert book
by Anna A. Creery; design by Pat Smith.

p.   cm.
Includes index.
ISBN 0-89865-627-3 : $7.95
1. Ice cream, ices, etc. 2. Desserts, Frozen. I. Title.
TX795.C74   1988   88-22941
641.8'62—dc 19   CIP

Printed in the United States of America

Table of Contents

Introduction

Frozen desserts are hot favorites in any dining setting from fancy restaurant to church social. With the more than 100 recipes included, you can make a variety—from rich ice cream to fresh fruit sorbet to calorie-wise yogurt—in any ice cream maker. The detail of our recipes is excellent, but we offer alternatives. When you feel even more creative, use our guidelines to develop "signature" recipes all your own.

Understanding ingredients is the key to changing recipes to suit your personal taste or dietary restrictions. We explain, for instance, that even in recipes that call for eggs, using them isn't mandatory. And, if you think an ice cream recipe that begins with a cooked custard sounds intriguing, but you don't have time to "stir constantly for ten minutes" as directed, try the recipe without cooking the custard.

Our frozen dessert recipes yield about one quart. It's easy to double them for a two-quart (half-gallon) ice cream maker or halve them for a one-pint (2 cup) one. Although many foods, such as cakes and breads, require exact ingredient measurements to work, ice cream proportions don't have to be as precise. The following chart will help when you want to halve our recipes. You'll notice that, for con-

1

venience, some of the measurements on the chart are not exactly halved.

MEASUREMENTS

QUART	PINT
1 tablespoon	1-½ teaspoons
¼ cup	2 tablespoons
⅓ cup	2-½ tablespoons
½ cup	¼ cup
⅔ cup	⅓ cup
¾ cup	6 tablespoons
1 cup	½ cup
1 egg	1 egg
3 eggs	1 or 2 eggs

All recipes have been tested in the Donvier® Ice Cream Maker, but any one can be made in any ice cream maker. The only change you'll need to make is in the amount your ice cream maker will hold, so follow the manufacturer's recommendation. Following are the instructions for best results using the Donvier® Ice Cream Maker.

Freezing the Chillfast™ Cylinder

1. **Adjust your freezer to the coldest possible setting!**
2. Remove the handle, lid and blade of the Donvier® Ice Cream Maker. Then remove the cylinder from the Donvier® outer case.
3. Wash the cylinder and dry thoroughly with a clean, dry cloth.
4. Make sure the plastic cylinder ring is placed on the cylinder *before* freezing.
5. Place the cylinder in the freezer. Freezer temperature must be at least 0 degrees F. If your freezer has a cold air vent, place the cylinder open end up directly in front of the air vent. If your freezer is a direct cooling type, place the cylinder directly on the floor of the freezer in an upright position.
6. Leave the cylinder in your freezer for at least 7 hours, preferably overnight.
7. Storing the Chillfast™ cylinder in your freezer at all times insures making ice cream at a moment's notice.

Making Ice Cream
in the Donvier®

Steps 2 through 8 should be done as quickly as possible to keep the cylinder properly chilled.

1. Take the cylinder out of the freezer.
2. Place the frozen cylinder in the Donvier® outer case, matching up the " ▲ " marks on the ring and outer case to prevent slipping.
3. Fit the bottom of the blade into the bottom of the cylinder.
4. Pour the blended ingredients into the cylinder.
5. Place the lid on the cylinder carefully aligning the " ▲ " marks on the cylinder ring with the "lock" tab on the lid. The hole in the lid should fit directly over the top of the blade.
6. Lock the lid by turning it in the direction indicated on the lid.
7. Immediately attach the handle and turn it clockwise *slowly* three or four times. (HINT: The arrow-shaped hole in the top of the blade points toward the knob at the end of the handle.)
8. Let the mixture sit for two or three minutes and turn the handle clockwise again two or three times. (If the freezing

of the ingredients makes turning diffi-
cult, turn the handle in the opposite
direction. Never force the blade. Work it
back and forth until the blade turns
freely.)

9. Continue this procedure for 20 minutes,
or until frozen.

10. The top of the turn handle has a small
plastic cap. This can be removed to plug
the opening in the top of the lid prior to
serving the contents. Do not allow
children to play with the cap.

11. Only use rubber, plastic or wooden
utensils to serve ice cream from the
Donvier®. Metal spoons may scratch
the cylinder.

12. Do not store ice cream in the cylinder. If
you must freeze leftover ice cream,
place it in plastic airtight containers.

If we may answer a question, solve a problem
or share a recipe write to:

Anna Creery
Donvier® Test Kitchen
562 Lynnhaven Parkway
Virginia Beach, Virginia 23452

Or call our TOLL FREE consumer line between the hours of 9 a.m. to 5 p.m., eastern
time.

Outside Virginia—800-334-4559
Inside Virginia—800-288-2367
Canada—800-387-9752

1

Quick &Easy Ice Creams

The Difference In Creams

Quick and easy is what the Donvier® Ice Cream Maker is all about. It requires no ice, no salt, no electricity and no endless cranking. The Donvier® Ice Cream Maker is homemade made simple. In some of these recipes, you'll need to heat a liquid to melt or dissolve another ingredient. Most, however, require no cooking, and delicious, homemade ice cream can be enjoyed within an hour.

Most ice creams are a combination of cream, milk, sugar, eggs and flavoring. You can use any cream you like, but the type of cream has a big impact on rich flavor and creamy texture. Creams with high percentages of butterfat are richer and creamier than those with low percentages. Heavy cream (available only in some parts of the country) has the highest butterfat percentage, at least 36 percent. In descending order are: whipping cream, at least 30 percent; coffee, table, light or 18 percent cream, at least 18 percent; and half-and-half, at least 10 percent. Most of our recipes include whipping cream and whole milk, but don't feel bound by those ingredients. Just make sure when you change a recipe to include the same total liquid measurement. If you want a richer ice cream, for instance:

▲ Original Recipe

1-½ cups whipping cream
1-½ cups milk

▲ Revised "Richer" Version

2 cups whipping cream
1 cup milk

Easy Vanilla
▲ **Ice Cream**

2 eggs
¾ cup sugar
1-¼ cups milk
2 cups whipping cream
1 teaspoon vanilla extract

In a blender or processor, combine
eggs, sugar and milk. Blend. Stir in
cream and vanilla. Makes about 1
quart.

Simply Great
▲ **Vanilla Ice Cream**

1 14-ounce can sweetened
    condensed milk
2 cups whipping cream
½ cup milk
1 teaspoon vanilla extract

In a mixing bowl, combine all
ingredients. Blend well. Makes
about 1 quart.

Honey Vanilla
▲ Ice Cream

1 cup milk
¾ cup honey
2 eggs
2 cups whipping cream

In a saucepan over medium heat, combine milk and honey. Stir occasionally until hot. Pour into blender or processor. With machine running, add eggs. Stir in cream. Chill thoroughly. Makes about 1 quart.

·Vanilla Ice Cream
▲ Base—For Variations

1 egg
¾ cup sugar
1-¼ cups milk
2 cups whipping cream

Note:

Read over variation recipe. It may omit sugar or differ in mixing.

Combine egg and sugar and whisk together. Stir in milk and cream. Add variation ingredients according to directions. This yields about 3-½ cups and allows for up to ¾ cup of your favorite chopped, crumbled or crushed cookie, candy or other flavor ingredient.

Variations:

Mint Chocolate Chip Ice Cream:
Add 1 teaspoon mint extract and ¾ cup mini chocolate chips to base. Optional: 1 drop green food coloring.

Cookies and Cream:
Add ¾ cup crushed cookie crumbs to base.

Candy and Cream:
Add ¾ cup finely chopped candy to base.

Cherry Vanilla Ice Cream:
Add ¾ cup pitted and finely chopped fresh Bing cherries, and ¼ teaspoon almond extract to base.

Easy Toffee Ice Cream:
Omit sugar. In a saucepan over low heat, melt 4 to 5 crushed toffee candy bars (about 5-½ ounces) in 1-¼ cups milk. Chill thoroughly. Combine toffee milk with egg and cream from base recipe.

Liqueur Ice Cream:
Add ½ cup of your favorite liqueur to base.

Very Chocolate
▲ Ice Cream

1 cup milk
1 egg
⅔ cup sugar
¾ cup unsweetened baking cocoa
2 cups whipping cream
1 teaspoon vanilla extract

In a blender or processor combine milk, egg, sugar and cocoa. Blend until smooth. Stir in cream and vanilla. Makes about 1 quart.

Simple Chocolate
▲ Ice Cream

½ cup sugar
1 cup milk
2 cups whipping cream
5 ounces semi-sweet baking
   chocolate, chopped

In a saucepan over medium heat, combine sugar, milk and cream. Stir occasionally until sugar dissolves and mixture is hot. Remove from heat and pour into blender or processor. Add chocolate. Process until chocolate is melted. Chill thoroughly. Makes about 1 quart.

Quick 'N' Easy
Strawberry
▲ Ice Cream

1 16-ounce package frozen sliced
    strawberries with sugar, thawed
2 cups whipping cream

In a blender or processor, puree
strawberries. Stir in cream. Makes
about 1 quart.

Strawberry
▲ Ice Cream

2-½ cups whole strawberries,
    fresh or frozen without
    sugar, thawed
½ cup milk
2 eggs
⅔ cup sugar
1 cup whipping cream
1 teaspoon vanilla extract

If using frozen fruit, measure while
frozen, then let thaw. In a blender or
processor, combine berries, milk
and eggs. Puree. Stir in sugar, cream
and vanilla. Makes about 1 quart.

No Cream
▲ Strawberry Ice Cream

1 12-ounce can evaporated milk
3 cups whole strawberries, fresh **or**
    frozen without sugar, thawed
¾ cup milk
¾ cup sugar
¼ teaspoon almond extract

If using a frozen fruit, measure while frozen, then let thaw. In a blender or processor, combine all ingredients. Puree. Makes about 1 quart.

No Cream
▲ Peach Ice Cream

Vary No Cream Strawberry Ice Cream above.

Substitute 2 cups sliced, peeled peaches for strawberries.

Cheesecake
▲ Ice Cream

1 8-ounce package cream cheese,
    room temperature
¾ cup sugar

2 eggs
2 teaspoons lemon juice
¼ teaspoon grated lemon zest
1 teaspoon vanilla extract
1 cup whipping cream
1 cup milk

In a mixing bowl, beat cream and sugar until fluffy. Add eggs one at a time, beating well after each addition. Add remaining ingredients and blend well. Makes about 1 quart.

Chocolate Chip Cheesecake
▲ Ice Cream

Vary Chesecake Ice Cream above.
Add ⅔ cup mini-chocolate chips.

Strawberry Cheesecake
▲ Ice Cream

Varry Cheesecake Ice Cream above.
Reduce sugar to ½ cup. Add ⅔ cup strawberry preserves after beating in eggs.

Peppermint
▲ Ice Cream

1-¾ cups milk
⅔ cup crushed peppermint candy
2 cups whipping cream

In a saucepan over medium heat, combine milk and candy. Heat and stir until candy dissolves, about 5 minutes. Cool slightly, then stir in cream. Chill thoroughly. Makes about 1 quart.

Serving Suggestion:
   Serve with Chocolate Crackle Sauce (page 102).

Banana
▲ Ice Cream

3 very ripe bananas
1 cup whipping cream
1 cup milk
2 eggs
2 teaspoons vanilla extract
½ cup sugar, optional

In a blender or processor, puree bananas and cream. Stir in remaining ingredients. Makes about 1 quart.

Pistachio
▲ Ice Cream

⅔ cup unsalted, shelled pistachios
1 egg
1 cup milk
¾ cup sugar
2 cups whipping cream
1 teaspoon vanilla extract
¼ teaspoon almond extract

In blender or processor, combine nuts, egg and milk. Blend until nuts are finely chopped. Mix in remaining ingredients. Makes about 1 quart.

Blueberry
▲ Ice Cream

2 cups blueberries, fresh **or**
    frozen without sugar, thawed
1 cup milk
1 cup whipping cream
¾ cup sugar

In a blender or processor, combine berries, milk, cream and sugar. Puree. Makes about 1 quart.

▲ Apricot Cream

3 ounces dried apricots
   (⅓ cup packed or
   about 15 apricot halves)
¾ cup sugar
2 cups water
1 cup whipping cream
1 cup milk
1 tablespoon lemon juice

In a saucepan over high heat, combine apricots, sugar and water. Bring to a boil. Reduce heat and simmer until fruit is very soft, about 15 minutes. Cool. Pour into blender or processor and puree. Stir in cream, milk and lemon juice. Chill thoroughly. Makes about 1 quart.

Cranberry
▲ Ice Cream

2 cups fresh cranberries
1 cup water
⅔ cup sugar
1 cup whipping cream

In a saucepan over medium heat, combine cranberries, water and sugar. Stir occasionally until sugar dissolves and cranberries have popped their skins. Let cool to room temperature. Pour into a blender or processor and puree. Stir in cream. Chill thoroughly. Makes about 1 quart.

Apple Spice
Ice Cream

1 12-ounce can apple juice
    concentrate, thawed
1 cup whipping cream
1-¼ cups milk
⅓ cup sugar
¼ teaspoon nutmeg
¼ teaspoon cinnamon

In a mixing bowl, combine all ingredients. Blend well. Makes about 1 quart.

Fresh Pear
▲ Ice Cream

2 cups peeled, chopped pears
   (about 2 large pears)
$\frac{2}{3}$ cup sugar
1 cup milk
1-$\frac{1}{2}$ cups whipping cream

In a saucepan over medium heat, combine pears, sugar and milk. Stir occasionally until sugar dissolves. Pour into blender or processor and puree. Stir in cream. Chill thoroughly. Makes about 1 quart.

Ginger Pear
▲ Ice Cream

Vary Fresh Pear Ice Cream above.

Add $\frac{1}{2}$ teapoon ground ginger.

▲ Raspberry Cream

1 16-ounce package frozen
   raspberries with sugar, thawed
2 cups whipping cream
1-$\frac{1}{2}$ teaspoons vanilla extract

In a blender or processor, combine raspberries and half of cream. Puree. Stir in remaining ingredients. Makes about 1 quart.

Substitution:
   2 10-ounce packages frozen raspberries with sugar.

▲ Raspberry Ice Cream

2 cups raspberries, fresh **or** frozen
   whole without sugar
1-¾ cups whipping cream
1 egg
¾ cup sugar
¾ cup milk

If using frozen berries, let thaw. Place berries, cream, egg and sugar in blender or processor. Blend until smooth. Add milk. Makes about 1 quart.

Substitution:
   1 10-ounce package raspberries, frozen with sugar. Decrease sugar to ¼ cup.

▲ Pineapple Cream

1 15-ounce can crushed pineapple
    in pineapple juice
2 cups whipping cream
¾ cup sugar

In a mixing bowl, combine all ingredients. Blend well. Makes about 1 quart.

▲ Pineapple Ice Cream

2 eggs
⅔ cup sugar
1 cup milk
1 cup whipping cream
1 15-ounce can crushed pineapple
    in pineapple juice

Whisk together eggs and sugar. Add remaining ingredients. Makes about 1 quart.

Toasted Almond
▲ Ice Cream

⅔ cup almonds, chopped
    (about 4 ounces)
2 eggs
⅔ cup sugar
1 cup milk

2 cups whipping cream
½ teaspoon almond extract

To toast nuts, place on a cookie sheet and bake at 350° for 5 to 8 minutes. Stir occasionally and watch closely. Cool thoroughly.

In a blender or processor, combine eggs, sugar and milk. Process until well mixed. Stir in cream, extract and nuts. Makes about 1 quart.

▲ Mocha Ice Cream

1-¼ cups milk
1-½ tablespoons instant
    coffee powder
⅓ cup unsweetened
    baking cocoa
⅔ cup sugar
2 eggs
2 cups whipping cream
1 teaspoon vanilla extract

In a saucepan over medium-high heat, heat milk until hot. Measure coffee, cocoa and sugar into a blender or processor. Add hot milk. Blend. With machine running, add eggs and continue to blend for 10 seconds. Stir in cream and vanilla. Chill thoroughly. Makes about 1 quart.

2

Cooked Custard
Ice Creams

*To Cook or
Not to Cook*

Technically, custard is a cooked mixture of eggs, milk and sugar. It often is used to enhance both flavor and richness in ice cream. If you don't have time to cook and then chill a custard, you can use the ingredients as specified in a recipe without cooking them. The shortcut won't produce exactly the same flavor or texture and you can't technically call it a custard base, but you'll be eating ice cream sooner.

Don't try to shortcut recipes that specify heating a liquid to dissolve an ingredient (such as sugar) or melt one (chocolate). If you're in a rush to finish, put the hot mixture in the freezer, stir occasionally and check every 15 minutes or so until it's cool. NEVER put a warm mixture into an ice cream maker.

We tested our recipes using an average weight saucepan. If you're using a heavy one, the heat can be increased. However, custards curdle if exposed to too much heat. We recommend using a wire whisk while stirring constantly. This results in a smoother custard and there is less chance of curdling because it more evenly exposes the custard to the heat.

French Vanilla Custard

½ vanilla bean
1 cup milk
¾ cup sugar
3 eggs
2 cups whipping cream

Slit the vanilla bean lengthwise. In a saucepan over medium heat, combine vanilla bean and milk. When milk is hot, remove bean and, with a knife, scrape out the inside of the bean into the milk. In a mixing bowl whisk together sugar and eggs. Whisking constantly, gradually add hot milk to egg mixture. Whisking constantly, add egg mixture back to saucepan. Stirring constantly, cook until slightly thickened, about 10 minutes. Stir in cream. Chill thoroughly. Makes about 1 quart.

Substitution:
Stir in 1 tablespoon vanilla extract after mixture has cooled.

Bittersweet
▲ Chocolate Ice Cream

4 ounces unsweetened
   baking chocolate
1 cup milk
3 eggs
½ cup sugar
2 cups whipping cream
1-½ teaspoons vanilla extract

In a saucepan over low heat, melt chocolate in milk, stirring occasionally. (There will be small bits of unmelted chocolate.) In a small bowl whisk together eggs and sugar. Whisking constantly, gradually add half of hot chocolate milk mixture to egg mixture. Stirring constantly, add egg mixture to saucepan. Increase heat to medium. Stirring constantly, cook until slightly thickened, about 8 minutes. Stir in cream and vanilla. Chill thoroughly. Makes about 1 quart.

Old Fashioned
▲ Strawberry Ice Cream

1 cup milk
1 cup sugar
2 eggs
2 cups whole strawberries, fresh,
   or frozen and thawed
1-½ cups whipping cream
1 teaspoon vanilla extract

In a saucepan over medium heat, heat milk until hot. In a small mixing bowl whisk together sugar and egg. Whisking constantly, gradually add hot milk to egg. Return mixture to saucepan over medium heat. Stirring constantly, cook until slightly thickened, about 8 minutes. Cool. In a blender or processor, puree fruit with cream. Stir into cooled custard. Add vanilla. Chill thoroughly. Makes about 1 quart.

Old Fashioned
▲ Peach Ice Cream

Vary Old Fashioned Strawberry Ice Cream above.

Substitute 1-½ cups sliced, peeled peaches for strawberries and ¼ teaspoon almond extract for vanilla.

Old Fashioned Lemon Custard
▲ Ice Cream

1 cup sugar
¼ cup flour
4 egg yolks
1-½ cups milk
½ teaspoon lemon extract
1-⅔ cups whipping cream

In a saucepan combine sugar and flour. Stir until flour is completely mixed with sugar and no lumps remain. Blend in egg yolks and milk. Place over medium heat. Stirring constantly, cook until slightly thickened, about 10 to 15 minutes. Stir in lemon extract and cream. Chill thoroughly. Makes about 1 quart.

Serving Suggestion:
    Serve in lemon shells. Slice large lemons lengthwise and ream out pulp.

▲ Lemon Ice Cream

1-½ tablespoons grated lemon zest
½ cup lemon juice
1 cup sugar
3 eggs

1 cup milk
1 cup whipping cream

In a saucepan over medium-high heat, combine zest, juice, sugar and eggs. Stirring constantly, cook until slightly thickened, about 8 minutes. Remove from heat. Stir in milk. Cool. Stir in cream. Chill thoroughly. Makes about 1 quart.

▲ Peach Ice Cream

2 eggs
¾ cup sugar
1 cup milk
2 cups sliced, peeled peaches
1-⅓ cups whipping cream
¼ teaspoon almond extract

In a saucepan over medium heat, combine eggs, sugar and milk. Stirring constantly, cook until slightly thickened, about 10 minutes. Cool slightly. In a blender or processor, combine cooled custard and peaches. Process until peaches are coarsely-chopped. Stir in cream and almond extract. Chill thoroughly. Makes about 1 quart.

▲ Caramel Ice Cream

1 cup sugar
1-½ cups milk
3 eggs
2 cups whipping cream

In a saucepan over medium heat, melt sugar without stirring constantly. This will take 20 to 30 minutes. (If you have a heavy saucepan, you may increase heat to medium-high.) When half of sugar has melted, stir to mix. In a small saucepan over high heat, heat milk until milk is hot. When all of sugar has melted, remove from heat. While stirring constantly, *gradually* add *small* amounts of hot milk to caramel sugar until all milk has been added. The caramel will foam and some will harden. In a mixing bowl whisk eggs. Whisking constantly, gradually add half of the hot caramel milk to the eggs. Stirring constantly, gradually add egg mixture back to saucepan. Place over medium heat. Stirring constantly, cook until mixture becomes smooth and hardened caramel melts, about 10 minutes. Cool. Stir in cream. Chill thoroughly. Makes about 1 quart.

Note:

Caramelized sugar is extremely hot. Use caution when making this recipe.

Peanut Butter
▲ Ice Cream

1-¾ cups milk
1 egg
½ cup sugar
1 cup crunchy peanut butter
1 cup whipping cream
1 teaspoon vanilla extract

In a saucepan over medium heat, heat milk until hot. In a small mixing bowl, whisk together egg and sugar. Whisking constantly, slowly add hot milk to the egg mixture. Return mixture to the saucepan. Stirring constantly, cook until slightly thickened, about 8 minutes. Remove from heat. Stir in peanut butter until blended. Stir in cream and vanilla. Chill thoroughly. Makes about 1 quart.

Virginia Peanut Butter Crunch
▲ Ice Cream

2 eggs
½ cup sugar
1 cup milk
½ cup peanut butter
1-½ cups whipping cream
1 teaspoon vanilla extract
⅔ cup roasted,
   salted peanuts, chopped

In a saucepan over medium heat, combine eggs, sugar and milk. Stirring constantly, cook until slightly thickened, about 10 minutes. Remove from heat. Add peanut butter and stir until melted. Stir in cream and vanilla. Chill thoroughly. Stir in peanuts right before freezing ice cream. Makes about 1 quart.

Peanut Butter Chocolate Chip
▲ Ice Cream

Vary Virginia Peanut Butter Crunch Ice Cream above.

Reduce chopped peanuts to ½ cup. Add peanuts and ½ cup chocolate chips right before freezing ice cream.

▲ Coffee Ice Cream

1-½ cups milk
2 tablespoons instant coffee powder
1 egg
¾ cup sugar
1-¾ cups whipping cream

In a saucepan over medium heat, heat milk until hot. Add coffee and stir until dissolved. In a small mixing bowl, whisk together egg and sugar until well blended. While whisking constantly, gradually add the hot milk mixture to the egg and sugar. Return mixture to saucepan over medium heat. Stirring constantly, cook until slightly thickened, about 8 minutes. Stir in cream. Chill thoroughly. Makes about 1 quart.

Rum Raisin
▲ Ice Cream

¾ cup raisins
½ cup rum **or** 2-½ teaspoons
    rum extract
1 cup milk
3 eggs
½ cup sugar
2 cups whipping cream

In a small glass bowl combine raisins and rum or extract. Cover and let stand about 3 hours. In a saucepan over medium heat, heat milk until hot. In a small mixing bowl, whisk together eggs and sugar. Whisking constantly, gradually add hot milk to egg. Return mixture to saucepan over medium heat. Stirring constantly, cook until slightly thickened, about 8 minutes. Stir in cream. Chill thoroughly. Add rum raisins right before beginning to freeze ice cream. Makes about 1 quart.

Butterscotch Pecan
▲ Ice Cream

¾ cup light brown sugar,
    firmly packed
2 tablespoons butter
2 tablespoons water
1 cup milk
2 eggs
1-¾ cups whipping cream
1 teaspoon vanilla extract
⅔ cup chopped pecans

In a saucepan over medium heat, combine brown sugar, butter and water. Stir occasionally until sugar is melted. In a mixing bowl, whisk together milk and eggs. While stirring constantly, gradually add melted sugar to milk and egg mixture. Return mixture to saucepan. Stirring constantly, cook until slightly thickened, about 8 minutes. Stir in cream and vanilla. Chill thoroughly. Stir in nuts right before freezing ice cream. Makes about 1 quart.

Coconut Cream Pie
▲ Ice Cream

1 cup milk
2 eggs
⅔ cup sugar
2 cups whipping cream
½ teaspoon vanilla extract
1 3-½ ounce can coconut

In a saucepan over medium heat combine milk, eggs and sugar. Stirring constantly, cook until slightly thickened, about 10 minutes. Stir in cream, vanilla and coconut. Chill thoroughly. Makes about 1 quart.

Toasted Coconut
▲ Ice Cream

Vary Coconut Cream Pie Ice Cream above by toasting coconut.

Spread coconut on a baking sheet and toast in a 350° oven. Stir frequently until golden brown, about 8 minutes. Cool thoroughly. Add to custard mixture right before freezing ice cream.

Cinnamon
▲ Ice Cream

¾ cup sugar
2 eggs
1-¼ cups milk
2 cups whipping cream
2 teaspoons ground cinnamon

In a saucepan over medium heat, combine sugar, eggs and milk. Stirring constantly, cook until slightly thickened, about 10 minutes. Remove from heat. Stir in cream and cinnamon. Cinnamon will mix in thoroughly when freezing ice cream. Chill thoroughly. Makes about 1 quart.

Maple Frost
▲ Ice Cream

2 eggs
$^2\!/_3$ cup maple syrup
1 cup milk
2 cups whipping cream
1-$^1\!/_2$ teaspoons vanilla extract

In a saucepan over medium heat, combine eggs, syrup and milk. Stirring constantly, cook until slightly thickened, about 8 minutes. Stir in cream and vanilla. Chill thoroughly. Makes about 1 quart.

Hazelnut
▲ Ice Cream

$^3\!/_4$ cup roasted hazelnuts
   (about 4 ounces)
2 eggs
$^2\!/_3$ cup sugar
1 cup milk
2 cups whipping cream
1 teaspoon vanilla extract

In a blender or processor, coarsely grind hazelnuts. In a saucepan over medium heat, combine nuts, eggs, sugar and milk. Stirring constantly, cook until slightly thickened, about 8 minutes. Stir in cream and vanilla. Chill thoroughly. Makes about 1 quart.

Jubilee Cherry
▲ Ice Cream

1-½ cups whipping cream
2 eggs
⅔ cup sugar
1 16-ounce can dark sweet
   pitted cherries, drained
1 cup milk
3 tablespoons kirsch or brandy **or**
   2 teaspoons brandy flavoring
¼ teaspoon almond extract

In a saucepan over medium heat, heat cream. In a mixing bowl, whisk together eggs and sugar. Stirring constantly, gradually add hot cream to egg mixture. Return to saucepan. Stirring constantly, cook until slightly thickened, about 8 minutes. Cool. Place remaining ingredients into blender or processor and coarsely chop cherries. Stir cherry mixture into cooled custard. Chill thoroughly. Makes about 1 quart.

Brandy Eggnog
▲ Ice Cream

1-¾ cups milk, divided
⅔ cup sugar
3 egg yolks
1-¾ cups whipping cream
¼ teaspoon nutmeg
¼ cup brandy **or** 2-½ teaspoons
    brandy flavoring

In a saucepan over medium heat, heat 1 cup milk. In a small bowl whisk together sugar and egg yolks. While stirring constantly, add hot milk to egg mixture. Return to saucepan. Stirring constantly, cook until slightly thickened, about 10 minutes. Remove from heat. Stir in remaining milk, cream, nutmeg and brandy. Chill thoroughly. Makes about 1 quart.

Frozen Pumpkin Cream

▲

1-½ cups milk
½ cup sugar
2 eggs
1 cup whipping cream
1 cup fresh cooked **or** solid
   pack canned pumpkin
¼ teaspoon cinnamon
½ teaspoon nutmeg

In a saucepan over medium heat, combine milk, sugar and eggs. Stirring constantly, cook until slightly thickened, about 10 minutes. Remove from heat. Whisk in cream, pumpkin, cinnamon and nutmeg. Chill thoroughly. Makes about 1 quart.

Serving Suggestion:
   Serve portions in individual baked pastry shells.

Banana Pudding
▲ **Ice Cream**

¾ cup sugar
2 tablespoons flour
1 cup milk
3 egg yolks
1 cup whipping cream
1 teaspoon vanilla extract
½ cup mashed banana
½ cup chopped banana
10 vanilla wafer cookies,
    broken into quarters

In a saucepan combine sugar and flour and mix well. Add milk, then whisk in egg yolks. Place over medium heat. Stirring constantly, cook until slightly thickened, about 10 minutes. Remove from heat and stir in cream, vanilla and bananas. Chill thoroughly. Right before beginning to freeze ice cream, stir in cookies. Makes about 1 quart.

White Chocolate
Chunk Ice Cream

9 ounces white chocolate, divided
1 cup milk
2 eggs
2 cups whipping cream
1 teaspoon vanilla extract

In a saucepan over low heat, melt 6 ounces of the white chocolate in milk. Stir occasionally. In a small mixing bowl, whisk eggs. When chocolate has melted, increase heat to medium. When milk is hot, whisking constantly, add half of hot milk mixture to eggs. Whisking constantly, add egg mixture back to saucepan. Stirring constantly, cook until slightly thickened, about 8 minutes. Stir in cream and vanilla. Cool. Finely chop remaining white chocolate and stir into mixture. Chill thoroughly. Makes about 1 quart.

White Chocolate
Ice Cream

Vary White Chocolate Chunk Ice Cream above.

Add all of white chocolate to milk to melt.

3

Sorbets & Ices

The Fruit
Taste Test

Although sorbets and ices both usually are made with fruit or fruit juice, sugar and water, they have a different texture. Ices have a somewhat granular, chunky texture, and sorbets a finer, smooth texture. For even a smoother one, some recipes include beaten egg whites.

Since sweetness of fresh fruit varies depending on ripeness, it's a good idea to taste the fruit before you begin the recipe. If the fruit is immature and too tart for your taste, add sugar. If the fruit is very ripe and sweet, decrease or omit the sugar. Remember, too, that freezing subdues sweetness, so the mixture will not be as sweet after it's frozen.

▲ Peach Sorbet

4 cups sliced, peeled peaches **or**
    1 16-ounce bag sliced peaches,
    frozen without sugar, thawed
2 cups water
1 tablespoon lemon juice
¼ teaspoon almond extract
½ cup sugar

In a blender or processor, combine peaches and water. Puree. Add remaining ingredients and stir to mix. Makes about 1 quart.

▲ Orange Sorbet

Zest of 1 medium orange
1 cup sugar
3 cups orange juice
½ cup water

In a blender or processor combine zest, sugar and 1 cup orange juice. Blend until zest is finely grated. Add remaining juice and water and stir to mix. Makes about 1 quart.

Three Berry
▲ Sorbet

½ cup sugar
½ cup water
1-⅓ cups blueberries **or**
    blackberries
1-⅓ cups strawberries
1-⅓ cups raspberries
1 cup orange juice

In a saucepan over high heat, combine sugar and water. Stir until sugar dissolves. Chill thoroughly. Combine sugar water, berries and juice in blender or processor. Puree. Makes about 1 quart.

Note:
    Use fresh berries or berries frozen whole without sugar. Use any proportion of berries to equal 4 cups.

▲ Raspberry Sorbet

3 cups fresh raspberries **or**
    1 12-ounce bag whole
    raspberries, frozen without sugar
½ cup water
⅔ cup sugar

2 egg whites
½ cup orange juice

In a saucepan over medium heat, combine raspberries, water and sugar. Stir until sugar is dissolved. Puree, then chill thoroughly. Beat egg whites until soft peaks form. Add orange juice to raspberries, then whisk in whites. Makes about 1 quart.

Substitution:
    2 10-ounce packages frozen raspberries with sugar. Thaw and puree. Do not add water or sugar.

▲ Raspberry Ice

3 10-ounce packages frozen
    raspberries with sugar
1 tablespoon lemon juice
Water

Let berries thaw. Place in colander and press out as much juice as possible. Yield should be 2 to 2-½ cups. Stir in lemon juice. Add water to equal 4 cups. Makes about 1 quart.

▲ Fraise Sorbet

3 cups whole strawberries, fresh **or**
    frozen without sugar, thawed
1-½ cups sparkling mineral water
⅓ cup sugar
⅔ cup strawberry liqueur

Place berries and mineral water in blender or processor. Puree. Stir in sugar and liqueur, stirring until sugar dissolves. Makes about 1 quart.

▲ Blueberry Sorbet

2 cups water
¾ cup sugar
3 cups blueberries, fresh **or**
    frozen without sugar

In a saucepan over high heat, combine water and sugar. Stir until sugar dissolves. In a blender or processor, combine sugar water and blueberries. Puree. Chill thoroughly. Makes about 1 quart.

Serving Suggestion:
  Serve with Lemon Curd Sauce
(page 105).

▲ Cranberry Sorbet

1 16-ounce can whole berry
  cranberry sauce
1-¾ cups water
2 tablespoons orange liqueur, like
Grand Marnier or Cointreau

Place all ingredients in blender or
processor and blend until mixed.
Makes about 1 quart.

Substitution:
  2 tablespoons orange juice concentrate
instead of liqueur.

Cranberry Citrus
▲ Sorbet

¾ cup water
1-½ cups fresh cranberries
1-½ cups sugar
1-½ cups orange juice

In a saucepan over medium-high heat, combine water, cranberries and sugar. Stir occasionally until cranberry skins pop open and sugar dissolves. Remove from heat and puree. Add orange juice. Chill thoroughly. Makes about 1 quart.

Serving Suggestion:
  Serve in reamed-out small orange halves.

▲ Apricot Sorbet

3 ounces dried apricots
    (⅓ cup packed or
    about 15 apricot halves)
2 cups water
Water
⅓ cup sugar

In a saucepan over high heat, combine apricots and 2 cups water. Bring to a boil, then reduce heat

and simmer 30 minutes. Pour contents of saucepan into blender or
processor and puree. Add water to
equal 4 cups mixture. Stir in sugar.
Chill thoroughly. Makes about 1
quart.

▲ Pineapple Sorbet

1 15-ounce can crushed pineapple
   in pineapple juice
1-2/3 cups unsweetened
   pineapple juice
3 tablespoons lemon juice
1/3 cup sugar

In a blender or processor, combine
all ingredients. Makes about 1 quart.

▲ Espresso Ice

4 tablespoons instant espresso
   coffee powder
3-⅔ cups boiling water
¾ cup sugar
1 teaspoon vanilla extract

Dissolve coffee in boiling water. Stir
sugar into coffee until dissolved.
Chill thoroughly. Stir in vanilla.
Makes about 1 quart.

Substitution:
   3 tablespoons regular instant coffee
powder.

Serving Suggestion:
   Serve with a dollop of whipped cream
and a sprinkle of unsweetened baking
cocoa.

▲ Kiwifruit Sorbet

2 cups water
½ cup sugar
6 kiwifruit
Water

In a saucepan over high heat, combine water and sugar. Stir until sugar dissolves. Cool. Peel and slice kiwifruit and sugar water in blender or processor. Puree. Add water to equal 4 cups. Chill thoroughly. Makes about 1 quart.

▲ Apple Sorbet

1 6-ounce can apple juice
    concentrate, thawed
½ cup water
3 cups apple juice
½ teaspoon cinnamon

Combine all ingredients. (The cinnamon will float on top but will mix in when freezing.) Makes about 1 quart.

▲ Lemon Ice

1 cup water
1-½ cups sugar
½ cup lemon juice
1 teaspoon grated lemon zest
2 cups cold water
Drop yellow food coloring,
   optional

In a small saucepan over high heat, combine water and sugar. Stir occasionally until sugar dissolves. Chill thoroughly. Combine sugar water with remaining ingredients. Makes about 1 quart.

▲ Lime Ice

1 cup water
1 cup sugar
½ cup lime juice
1 teaspoon grated lime zest
2 cups cold water
Drop green food coloring,
    optional

In a small saucepan over high heat, combine water and sugar. Stir occasionally until sugar dissolves. Chill thoroughly. Combine with remaining ingredients. Makes about 1 quart.

4

Frozen
Yogurts &
Sherbets

Blender,
Food Processor or
Electric Mixer?

Homemade frozen yogurt is totally different from commercial products, which include concentrated fruit purees, flavoring, emulsifiers and stabilizers not available to the average consumer.

For a light, satisfying compromise between ice cream and sorbet, try sherbet—usually fruit based and always made with milk instead of cream.

Although our recipes often specify using a blender or food processor for speed, they also can be mixed with an electric beater or by hand with a whisk. Recipes that include pureed fruit, however, should be pureed in a blender or processor.

▲ Frozen Lemon Yogurt

3 8-ounce containers lemon yogurt
1 cup milk
1 small box (4 ½-cup serving size)
  sugar-free lemon gelatin

In a mixing bowl, combine all
ingredients. Mix well. Makes about
1 quart.

▲ Banana Yogurt

2 cups chopped bananas
1 16-ounce carton (2 cups)
  vanilla yogurt
⅔ cup milk
¼ cup light corn syrup
½ teaspoon vanilla extract

In a blender or processor, combine
all ingredients. Puree. Makes about
1 quart.

Raspberry Yogurt

1 16-ounce carton (2 cups)
   vanilla yogurt
1 16-ounce package frozen
   raspberries with sugar, thawed

In a blender or processor, combine all ingredients. Blend well. Makes about 1 quart.

Substitution:
   2 10-ounce packages frozen raspberries with sugar.

Banana Orange Yogurt

1 16-ounce carton (2 cups)
   vanilla yogurt
1 cup orange juice
1 cup mashed banana
¼ cup milk
¼ cup light corn syrup

In a mixing bowl, combine all ingredients. Mix well. Makes about 1 quart.

▲ Pineapple Yogurt

3 8-ounce cartons (3 cups)
   pineapple yogurt
1 cup milk
1 small box (4 ½-cup servings)
   sugar-free pineapple gelatin

In a mixing bowl, combine all ingredients. Mix well. Makes about 1 quart.

▲ Frozen Fruit Yogurt

1 16-ounce carton (2 cups)
   vanilla yogurt
1-⅓ cups milk
⅔ cup fruit preserves

In a mixing bowl, combine all ingredients. Mix well. Makes about 1 quart.

Note:
   If a sweeter version is preferred, add ¼ cup light corn syrup.

▲ Strawberry Yogurt

1 16-ounce package frozen sliced
   strawberries with sugar, thawed
1 16-ounce carton (2 cups)
   vanilla yogurt

In a blender or processor, puree
strawberries. Stir in yogurt. Makes
about 1 quart.

▲ Lemonade Sherbet

3 cups milk
1 cup frozen lemonade concentrate
¼ cup sugar
Drop yellow food coloring,
   optional

Combine all ingredients and stir
until sugar dissolves. Mixture will
look curdled. Makes about 1 quart.

Note:
   You will need to buy a 12-ounce can of
frozen lemonade concentrate. Freeze leftover concentrate or make into lemonade.

Lime Sherbet

2-2/3 cups milk
7/8 cup lime juice (7/8 cup = 1 cup
    minus 2 tablespoons)
1 cup sugar
Drop green food coloring,
    optional

Combine all ingredients and stir
until sugar dissolves. Mixture will
look curdled. Makes about 1 quart.

Orange Sherbet

1/2 cup water
1 cup sugar
1 6-ounce can frozen orange juice
    concentrate, thawed
2-1/4 cups milk

In a saucepan over high heat, combine water and sugar. Stir until sugar
is dissolved. Chill thoroughly. Stir in
orange juice and milk. Makes about
1 quart.

Limeade Sherbet

Vary Orange Sherbet above.

Substitute 1 6-ounce can frozen
limeade concentrate for orange
juice.

Chocolate Sherbet
▲ L'Orange

¼ cup water
3 ounces unsweetened
    baking chocolate
1 cup sugar
2-¼ cups milk
½ cup orange juice
1 teaspoon grated orange zest
2 tablespoons orange liqueur,
    like Grand Marnier **or** Cointreau

In a saucepan over low heat, combine water, chocolate and sugar. Stir occasionally until chocolate melts. Heat milk in a saucepan over medium heat. When milk is hot and chocolate is melted, gradually stir milk into chocolate. Cool. Add orange juice, zest and liqueur. Chill thoroughly. Makes about 1 quart.

Substitution:
    2 tablespoons orange juice concentrate instead of liqueur.

Marmalade Sherbet

1-¾ cups orange juice
½ cup orange marmalade
½ cup sugar
1-½ cups milk

In a blender or processor, combine juice, marmalade and sugar. Process until well mixed. Add milk. Makes about 1 quart.

5

Special Desserts for Special Diets

Substitutions and Equivalents

Even if you're concerned about cutting calories, lowering cholesterol consumption and eliminating dairy products or other food allergies, there's a varied choice of frozen desserts for you. In addition to the following recipes, try the sorbets and ices. These are very easy to fit into any diet as they are usually just fruit, water and sugar. To lower calories, use this chart as a guide for substituting artificial sweetener for sugar.

If you're using a recipe that requires cooking, do NOT add artificial sweetener until mixture has cooled. When the recipe (for sorbet or ice) specifies heating liquid to dissolve sugar, omit the heating and just stir sweetener in until thoroughly dissolved.

Sugar		Low-Calorie Sweetener
2 teaspoons	=	1 packet
¼ cup	=	6 packets
⅓ cup	=	8 packets
½ cup	=	12 packets
⅔ cup	=	16 packets
¾ cup	=	18 packets
1 cup	=	24 packets

When recipes include other foods you must avoid, simply change the recipe. Granted, substitutions will alter taste and texture, but they will not keep mixtures from freezing as long as you remember one thing: keep the volume the same. In other words, when one ingredient is eliminated, it must be replaced by the same amount of another. For example, if a recipe calls for 3 eggs (which measure 3 tablespoons each), but you want to reduce the cholesterol, replace the egg with 9 tablespoons of milk, water, fruit or other ingredient appropriate to the specific recipe.

▲ Watermelon Sorbet

1 cup water
16 packets low-calorie sweetener
3-½ cups chopped watermelon,
    seeded and firmly packed

In a blender or processor, combine water, sweetener and watermelon. Puree. Makes about 1 quart.

▲ Pumpkin Ice "Cream"

2 cups skim milk
½ cup nonfat dry milk
½ cup sugar
2 eggs
1 cup fresh cooked or solid pack
    canned pumpkin
¼ teaspoon ground cinnamon
¼ teaspoon nutmeg

In a saucepan, whisk together milk, dry milk, sugar and eggs. Stirring constantly, cook over medium heat for 8 minutes. Remove from heat and whisk in pumpkin and spices. Chill thoroughly. Makes about 1 quart.

Non-Dairy
Berry Dessert

2 cups soy "milk"
2 cup fresh strawberries
⅔ cup sugar
½ teaspoon almond extract

In a blender or processor, combine soy milk and berries. Puree. Add sugar and almond extract. Stir until sugar dissolves. Makes about 1 quart.

Pear Sorbet

3 large ripe pears, peeled,
    cored and sliced
2 cups water
⅓ cup sugar
2 tablespoons lemon juice
Water

In a saucepan over medium heat, combine pears, 2 cups water and sugar. Stir until sugar dissolves. Pour into blender or processor and puree. Add lemon juice and water to equal 4 cups. Chill thoroughly. Makes about 1 quart.

Amaretti 'N' Cream

2-½ cups lowfat milk
1-½ cups part skim ricotta cheese
¾ cup sugar
2 cinnamon sticks
½ cup crumbled Amaretti cookies

In a saucepan over medium heat, combine milk, cheese, sugar and cinnamon sticks. Stir constantly until mixture begins to steam. Remove from heat and cool. Remove and discard cinnamon stickets. Pour mixture into blender or processor. Blend until smooth. Chill thoroughly. Add crumbled cookies to mixture right before freezing ice cream. Makes about 1 quart.

Pineapple
▲ Almond Sorbet

2 cups fresh pineapple chunks,
   packed
2 cups unsweetened pineapple juice
¼ teaspoon almond extract

In a blender or processor, puree
pineapple chunks and juice. Stir in
extract. Makes about 1 quart.

Serving Suggestion:
  Garnish with sliced almonds

Toasted Coconut-Honey Sherbet

2/3 cup freshly grated coconut, toasted
2-1/3 cups lowfat milk
2/3 cup honey
1/4 teaspoon coconut flavoring
2 egg whites, stiffly beaten

To toast coconut, spread on a cookie sheet and bake in a 350° oven until golden brown, about 8 minutes. Stir frequently and watch closely. Cool thoroughly.

In a saucepan over medium heat, combine milk and honey. Stir until honey dissolves, about 5 minutes. Remove from heat. Chill thoroughly. Stir in coconut flavoring, egg whites and coconut. Makes about 1 quart.

▲ Mulled Cider Sorbet

2-2/3 cups fresh apple cider,
    divided
½ cup honey
1 tart apple, peeled, cored
    and sliced
1 stick cinnamon
¼ teaspoon nutmeg

In a saucepan over medium-low heat, combine 2/3 cup cider, honey, apple slices and spices. Simmer 10 minutes. Cool. Remove cinnamon stick. Combine apple and juices with remaining cider. Puree. Chill thoroughly. You should have 4 cups; if not, add cider to equal 4 cups. Makes about 1 quart.

▲ Fruit Ice "Cream"

½ cup nonfat dry milk
2 cups skim milk
1 egg, slightly beaten
1 cup pureed fruit, any kind
10 packets low-calorie sweetener

Dissolve dry milk in fluid milk. Whisk in egg. Stir in fruit and sugar substitute. Makes about 1 quart.

6

Fun,
Fanciful,
Exotic

Miscellany

When you're in the mood to experiment, there's a whole potpourri of ideas here. Chocolate Truffle Ice Cream and Cream L'Orange have only three ingredients each.

If your ice cream yearning has an Italian accent, try one of the gelato recipes based on Italy's rich, dense, almost pudding-like ice cream. The intense flavor, typical of classic gelato, is so pronounced in our Chocolate Gelato that it's a chocoholic's dream.

Hungry for exotic fare, fun food, or a combination of favorites? Satisfy the craving with Turkish Fig, Piña Colada, White Chocolate Macadamia Nut or Pumpkin-Caramel Swirl.

For a grande finale, try Chocolate Raspberry Truffle Ice Cream made with raspberry liqueur. If you'd rather not use alcohol in it (or any other recipe), simply replace it with an equal amount of milk or cream unless you're making sorbet. Then, water is the replacement ingredient.

Above all, experiment and enjoy.

Vanilla Bean
▲ Ice Cream

3 cups whipping cream
½ cup milk
1 cup sugar
1 vanilla bean, slit lengthwise

In a saucepan over medium-low heat, combine all ingredients. Stir occasionally until sugar dissolves. Cool slightly. With a small knife, scrape tiny black vanilla seeds from bean into cream. Discard bean. Chill thoroughly. Makes about 1 quart.

Serving Suggestion:
   Serve with Caramel Sauce (pages 103 or 104).

Chocolate Raspberry
▲ Truffle Ice Cream

1-½ cups raspberries, fresh
   or frozen whole without sugar
3 tablespoons sugar
½ cup raspberry liqueur
½ cup sugar
½ cup unsweetened baking cocoa
1 cup milk
2 eggs
1-½ cups whipping cream

Place berries in a shallow bowl.
Combine 3 tablespoons sugar and
liqueur and stir until sugar is dissolved. Pour over berries and stir to
mix. Cover and refrigerate.

In a saucepan combine ½ cup sugar
and cocoa. Stir until well mixed. Stir
in milk, then whisk in eggs. Place
over medium heat. Stirring constantly, cook until slightly thickened,
about 8 minutes. Remove from heat.
Stir in cream. Chill thoroughly.
Using a slotted spoon, remove raspberries from liqueur and juices. Set
raspberries aside. Add liqueur and
juices to ice cream mixture. Begin
to freeze ice cream. When half of
mixture has frozen, remove handle
and lid. Add raspberries. Replace lid

Chocolate Truffle
▲ Ice Cream

12 ounces semi-sweet
 baking chocolate
2 cups whipping cream
1 cup milk

In a heavy saucepan over low heat, melt chocolate. In another saucepan over medium heat, heat cream until hot. When chocolate is melted, gradually stir in cream. Stir in milk. Chill thoroughly. Makes about 1 quart.

and handle. Continue to freeze to desired consistency. Makes about 1 quart.

Substitution:
 1 10-ounce package raspberries frozen with sugar instead of raspberries and 3 tablespoons sugar.

Chocolate Gelato

¾ cup unsweetened baking cocoa
¾ cup sugar
1 cup milk
2 eggs, slightly beaten
1-½ cups whipping cream

In a saucepan combine cocoa and sugar. Stir until well mixed. Gradually add milk, making a paste. Whisk in eggs. Place over medium heat and cook and stir until steaming, about 8 to 10 minutes. Stir in cream. Chill thoroughly. Makes about 1 quart.

White Chocolate Gelato

2 eggs
1 cup milk
1-¾ cups whipping cream
9 ounces white chocolate

In a saucepan over medium heat, combine eggs, milk and cream. Stirring constantly, cook until slightly thickened, about 10 minutes. Remove from heat. Break white chocolate into pieces and add to hot cream mixture. Stir until melted. Chill thoroughly. Makes about 1 quart.

White Chocolate Macadamia Nut ▲ Ice Cream

⅔ cup chopped macadamia nuts, toasted
½ cup sugar
3 eggs
1-¼ cups milk
6 ounces white chocolate
1-¼ cups whipping cream

To toast nuts, place on a cookie sheet and bake at 350° for 5 to 8 minutes. Stir occasionally and watch closely. Cool thoroughly.

In a saucepan over medium heat, combine sugar, eggs and milk. Stirring constantly, cook until slightly thickened, about 8 minutes. Reduce heat to low and add white chocolate. Stir occasionally until melted. Remove from heat. Add cream. Chill thoroughly. Stir in nuts right before freezing ice cream. Makes about 1 quart.

Bananas Foster
Ice Cream

¼ cup butter
¼ cup light brown sugar,
    firmly packed
¼ cup sugar
2 cups finely chopped bananas
¼ cup light rum **or** 1-¼ teaspoons
    rum extract
2 cups whipping cream

In a saucepan over medium-high heat, combine butter and sugars. Add bananas when butter has melted. Stir to mix. When mixture comes to a simmer, add rum. (If using rum extract, do not add at this time.) Stirring occasionally, simmer until mixture thickens slightly, about 3 minutes. Remove from heat. (Add extract.) Stir in cream. Chill thoroughly. Makes about 1 quart.

▲ Cantaloupe Cream

3-½ cups cantaloupe chunks
1 cup half and half
½ cup sugar
¼ teaspoon almond extract

In a blender or processor, puree cantaloupe with cream. Stir in sugar and extract. Makes about 1 quart.

▲ Cream L'Orange

2-¾ cups whipping cream
1 cup orange marmalade
2 tablespoons orange liqueur,
    like Grand Marnier or Cointreau

In a mixing bowl, whisk together cream and marmalade until well mixed. Stir in liqueur. Makes about 1 quart.

Serving Suggestion:
  Serve with Raspberry-Orange Sauce (page 107).

Pumpkin Caramel
▲ Swirl Ice Cream

2 eggs
½ cup sugar
1 cup milk
1 cup fresh cooked **or** solid-pack
    canned pumpkin
½ teaspoon cinnamon
¼ teaspoon nutmeg
1 cup whipping cream
6 ounces caramel candies, about 18
⅓ cup milk

In a saucepan over medium heat, combine eggs, sugar and milk. Stirring constantly, cook until slightly thickened, about 10 minutes. Remove from heat. Whisk in pumpkin, spices and cream. Chill thoroughly.

In a small saucepan over low heat, combine caramels and milk. Stir occasionally until melted. Let cool to room temperature. Begin freezing ice cream. When ice cream is frozen to desired consistency, remove handle, lid and blade. Pour caramel sauce over ice cream and fold caramel into ice cream. Makes about 1 quart.

▲ Amaretto Cream

⅔ cup coarsely ground almonds,
 toasted
1 egg
¾ cup sugar
1 cup milk
2 cups whipping cream
½ teaspoon almond extract
¼ cup almond liqueur,
 like amaretto

To toast nuts, place on a cookie sheet and bake at 350° for 5 to 8 minutes. Stir occasionally and watch closely. Cool thoroughly.

In a saucepan over medium heat, combine egg, sugar and milk. Stirring constantly, cook until slightly thickened, about 10 minutes. Remove from heat. Stir in cream, extract and liqueur. Chill thoroughly. Stir in nuts right before freezing ice cream. Makes about 1 quart.

Creme De Framboise

1 10-ounce package raspberries
frozen with sugar, thawed
½ cup raspberry liqueur
2 cups whipping cream
½ cup milk

In a mixing bowl, combine raspberries and liqueur. Stir in cream and milk. Makes about 1 quart.

Turkish Fig
▲ Ice Cream

6 ounces dried figs, about 10
1 cup water
½ cup sugar
2 cups milk
¾ cup whipping cream
1 teaspoon rum extract

Cut figs in quarters. In a small saucepan over high heat, combine figs and water. Bring to a boil. Reduce heat to a simmer and cover with a tight-fitting lid. Simmer until figs have softened, about 30 minutes. With a slotted spoon, remove figs and place in blender or processor. Add sugar to remaining water and stir until dissolved. Add sugar water and milk to figs. Puree. Stir in cream and extract. Chill thoroughly. Makes about 1 quart.

Piña Colada
▲ Ice Cream

1 15-ounce can cream of coconut
1 15-ounce can crushed pineapple
   in pineapple juice
1 cup whipping cream
½ teaspoon plus ¼ teaspoon
   rum extract

If coconut is congealed, place opened can in a pan of warm water until melted. Pour into mixing bowl and add remaining ingredients. Stir to mix. Chill thoroughly. Makes about 1 quart.

▲ Heavenly Hash

1 cup milk
1 egg
½ cup sugar
⅔ cup unsweetened baking cocoa
1-½ cups whipping cream
⅓ cup each: chopped almonds,
 mini-chocolate chips and
 miniature marshmallows

In a blender or processor, combine milk, egg, sugar and cocoa. Blend until smooth. Stir in remaining ingredients. Makes about 1 quart.

7

Sauces

*Ripening
Ice Cream*

Homemade ice cream is about as good as dessert gets...unless you want to gild the lily with a sauce or topping.

Before you do that, it's best to let the ice cream ripen first so flavors can mellow and the texture will firm up more to keep from melting too quickly under hot toppers. In the Donvier® Ice Cream Maker let it ripen for 30 minutes or longer, turning 2 or 3 times every 10 to 15 minutes. (Do NOT return to freezer.) For other ice cream makers, follow the manufacturer's directions for ripening.

Bittersweet
▲ Fudge Sauce

½ cup unsweetened baking cocoa
½ cup sugar
½ cup whipping cream
¼ cup butter

In a saucepan, stir cocoa and sugar until well mixed. Add cream and butter and place over medium-low heat. Stir occasionally until butter is melted and mixture is smooth, about 10 minutes. Makes about 1 cup.

Chocolate
▲ Fudge Sauce

Vary Bittersweet Fudge Sauce above.
Increase sugar to ¾ cup.

Chocolate
▲ Crackle Sauce

6 ounces semi-sweet
   baking chocolate
6 tablespoons butter

In a saucepan over low heat, combine ingredients. Stir occasionally
until melted, about 15 minutes.
Makes about 1 cup.

Note:
   This sauce becomes hard when poured
over ice cream.

▲ Chocolate Sauce

¾ cup whipping cream
7 ounces semi-sweet
   baking chocolate

In a saucepan over low heat, heat
cream until hot. Remove from heat.
Add chocolate. Stirring occasionally,
let sit until chocolate is melted and
mixture is smooth. Makes about 1-½
cups.

Quick 'N' Easy
▲ Caramel Sauce

7 ounces caramel candies, about 22
½ cup milk

In a saucepan over low heat, combine ingredients. Stir occasionally until melted, about 20 minutes. Cool slightly before serving. Makes about 1 cup.

▲ Caramel Sauce

1 cup sugar
2 tablespoons water
½ cup whipping cream

In a saucepan over medium-high heat, combine sugar and water. Stir until all of sugar is moistened. Stirring occasionally, let boil until golden in color, about 10 to 15 minutes. Remove from heat. While stirring constantly, *slowly* add small amounts of cream. Return saucepan to low heat and stir occasionally until any lumps of hardened caramel have melted. Let cool, then taste. If caramel flavor is too strong, stir in additional cream. Makes about 1 cup.

Note:
Caramelized sugar is extremely hot. Use caution when making this recipe.

Apricot Brandy Sauce

1 12-ounce jar apricot preserves
1 tablespoon lemon juice
2 tablespoons brandy **or**
    2 teaspoons brandy flavoring
2 tablespoons water

In a saucepan over low heat, combine all ingredients. Stir occasionally until heated through and well blended. Cool slightly before serving. Makes about 1-1/3 cups.

Lemon Curd Sauce

1/4 cup lemon juice
3/4 cup sugar
6 tablespoons butter
2 eggs, slightly beaten

In a saucepan over medium heat, combine lemon juice, sugar and butter. Stir occasionally until butter is melted. Remove from heat. While stirring vigorously, gradually add eggs. Return saucepan to medium heat. Stirring constantly, cook until mixture thickens slightly, about 8 minutes. Serve warm or cold. Makes about 1-1/2 cups.

Butterscotch Sauce

1 cup light brown sugar,
   firmly packed
3 tablespoons butter
$\frac{2}{3}$ cup whipping cream **or**
   1 5-ounce can evaporated milk
$\frac{1}{2}$ teaspoon vanilla extract

In a saucepan over medium heat, combine sugar, butter and cream. Stir occasionally until sugar dissolves and butter is melted, about 5 to 8 minutes. Cool slightly, then stir in vanilla. Makes about 1-$\frac{1}{3}$ cups.

Raspberry-Orange Sauce

1 tablespoon cornstarch
¼ cup sugar
1 10-ounce package frozen
    raspberries with sugar, thawed
½ teaspoon grated orange zest
2 tablespoons orange juice

In a small bowl, combine cornstarch and sugar. In a saucepan over medium heat, place raspberries. Add sugar mixture, zest and juice. Stir occasionally until mixture thickens and turns from cloudy to clear. Cool slightly before serving. Makes about 1-⅓ cups.

8

Frozen Drinks

The Proof is in the Ice Cream

Alcohol inhibits freezing, so anything that includes alcohol is a softer texture than it would be without it. The recipes in this chapter all include alcohol and can be served as drinks or frozen longer and eaten with a spoon.

Frozen Brandy
▲ Alexander

2 cups whipping cream
1 cup milk
½ cup creme de cacao
⅓ cup brandy

In a mixing bowl, combine cream, milk, cream de cacao and brandy. Mix well. Makes about 1 quart.

▲ # Frozen Piña Coladas

1 8-ounce can cream of coconut
2-½ cups unsweetened
   pineapple juice
½ cup dark rum

If coconut is congealed, place opened can in a pan of warm water until melted. Combine all ingredients. Makes about 1 quart.

Frozen Strawberry
▲ Daiquiris

3 cups whole strawberries
1 cup water
⅔ cup sugar
⅓ cup lime juice
¾ cup light rum

In a blender or processor, combine strawberries and water. Puree. Stir in remaining ingredients, stirring until sugar dissolves. Makes about 1 quart.

Note:
   Please read paragraph on page 50 regarding fresh fruit.

Frozen Peach
▲ Daiquiris

Vary Frozen Strawberry Daiquiris above.

Substitute 2 cups sliced, peeled peaches for strawberries. Add ½ teaspoon almond extract.

Frozen Banana
▲ Daiquiris

Vary Frozen Strawberry Daiquiris above.

Substitute 2 cups sliced bananas for strawberries.

▲ Frozen Margaritas

2-⅓ cups water
½ cup lime juice
¾ cup triple sec
⅔ cup dark tequila

Combine all ingredients. Makes about 1 quart.

▲ Frozen Strawberry Margaritas

Vary Frozen Margaritas above.

Omit water. Add 4 cups whole strawberries, pureed, and ⅓ cup sugar.

▲ Frosty Spiked Nog

2 eggs
$2/3$ cup sugar
$1/3$ cup bourbon
$1/3$ cup light rum
1 cup milk
1-$1/2$ cups whipping cream

In a mixing bowl, combine eggs, sugar, bourbon, rum and milk. Whisk until eggs are blended and sugar is dissolved. Stir in cream. Makes about 1 quart.

▲ Viennese Cream Coffee

$2/3$ cup sugar
1-$1/3$ cups strong brewed coffee
1-$1/3$ cups whipping cream
$2/3$ cup brandy

Dissolve sugar in coffee. Chill thoroughly. Stir in cream and brandy. Makes about 1 quart.

▲ Irish-Mexican Coffee

$1/3$ cup sugar
1 cup brewed coffee
1 cup milk
1 cup whipping cream
$1/3$ cup coffee liqueur,
    like Kahlua
$1/4$ cup Irish whiskey

Dissolve sugar in coffee. Chill thoroughly. Add remaining ingredients. Makes about 1 quart.

Frosted
▲ Almond Cream

$1/2$ cup sugar
$1-1/2$ cups milk
$1-1/2$ cups whipping cream
$2/3$ cup almond liqueur,
    like amaretto

Combine all ingredients and stir until sugar is dissolved. Makes about 1 quart.

Cordially Yours

Cordials and liqueurs are naturals for flavoring ice creams and the lower alcohol content does not inhibit freezing as dramatically as liquors such as rum or brandy.

Until recently, making cordials and liqueurs at home has meant a one- to six-month wait for ageing to take the sharp bite off alcohol and give flavors time to develop. With the Coridally Yours™ by Donvier® you now can age them overnight. The compact, easy-to-use appliance makes sparkling, clear fruit syrups for waffles, pancakes or ice cream toppings; flavored oils, such as sesame and hot chili, to enliven Oriental dishes; and herb- or fruit-flavored vinegars to perk up just about any dish. The Cordially Yours™ will even age that leftover bottle of wine that's been stuck in the back of the fridge for who-knows-how long into wine vinegar.

Several of our frozen desserts include raspberry liqueur, which you can make with the following recipe, almost as easily as you can buy it. Let the ingredients age the old-fashioned way for four months or age in the Cordially Yours™ for only eight hours.

Raspberry Liqueur

1 pint raspberries **or** 3 cups
   raspberries, frozen whole
   without sugar
3 cups vodka
2 cups sugar

Place raspberries in inner pot. In a
pitcher, combine vodka and sugar.
Stir until sugar is dissolved. Pour
into inner pot. Set timer for 8 hours.
(Without Cordially Yours™ age 4
months.)

Almond Liqueur

1 dried apricot
1 tablespoon plus 1 teaspoon
   almond extract
1 cup water
1-¼ cups sugar
1-¼ cups vodka
1-¼ cups brandy

Place apricot in inner pot. In a
pitcher, combine remaining ingredients. Stir until sugar is dissolved.
Pour into inner pot. Set timer for 6
hours. (Without Cordially Yours™
age 3 months.)

▲ Coffee Liqueur

2 cups boiling water
¼ cup plus 3 tablespoons instant
   coffee powder
3-½ cups sugar
2 cups vodka
1 vanilla bean, split

Pour boiling water into inner pot.
Add instant coffee and stir until
dissolved. Add sugar and stir until
sugar is dissolved. Add vodka and
vanilla bean. Stir to mix. Set timer
for 8 hours. (Without Cordially Yours™
age 4 months.)

▲ Orange Liqueur

⅓ cup orange zest
1 cup sugar
4 cups cognac **or** brandy

Place zest in inner pot. In a pitcher,
combine sugar and cognac. Stir until
sugar is dissolved. Pour into inner
pot. Set timer for 8 hours. (Without
Cordially Yours™ age 4 months.)

▲ Clear Fruit Syrup

¾ cup water
2 cups sugar
4 cups fruit **or** 1 1-pound bag fruit,
frozen without sugar

Place water and sugar in a saucepan over high heat. Stir until sugar is dissolved. Place fruit in inner pot. Pour sugar water over fruit. Set timer for 4 hours. Strain out fruit if desired. Refrigerate. Will keep for one month in the refrigerator. Yield: 2-½ cups.

Index